Brown Rabbit's Shape Book

Alan Baker

KINGFISHER

KINGFISHER
An imprint of Kingfisher Publications Plc
New Penderel House, 283-288 High Holborn
London WC1V 7HZ

First published in paperback by Kingfisher 1995
This edition published in 1998
4 6 8 10 9 7 5
4TR/1000/TWP/PW/150ARM
Originally published in hardback by Kingfisher 1994

A CIP catalogue record for this book
is available from the British Library

ISBN 1 85697 405 7

Printed in Singapore

One day a parcel arrived
for Brown Rabbit.
It had bright red triangles
on the wrapping paper.

The card was
the shape of a
rectangle. It said
"To Brown Rabbit".

To Brown x
Rabbit x x

Rabbit took off the paper.
Underneath was a
square box. Rabbit
lifted the lid.

Inside was
a tube ...

... with a circle shape top.
Rabbit opened it.

Out tumbled
five flat floppy
balloons,
all different
colours.

Lovely balloons,
just waiting
to be blown up.

Rabbit blew up the red balloon.
It was big and round like a ball.

Whoosh! Away it flew.

The orange balloon was oval-shaped like an egg.

Whoosh! It flew off.

The green balloon was l o n g
and sausage-shaped.
Rabbit couldn't hold it.
Whoo-whoosh!
Off it went.

The purple balloon
was smaller and
shaped like a pear.

One more puff, thought Rubbit.
Then BANG! It burst.

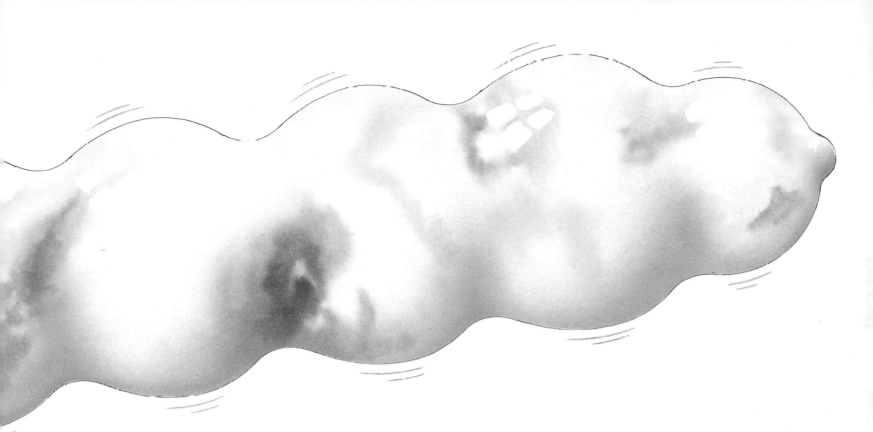

The last balloon was all colours,
l o n g and lumpy-bumpy.

Whoosh! Blast off!

Whoo ... Whoo ... Whoo-oosh!

Goodbye balloon shapes.
I'm all out of puff,
thought Rabbit.

He tidied up the balloons,
the tube, the box
and the paper.

Then rabbit-shaped Rabbit
fell fast asleep on top.